Float The Day

Chuck Johnson

FLOAT THE DAY

First Edition
ISBN: 978-1-7350434-0-1
Library of Congress Control Number: 2020908558

This book is a collection of things I've written over the last few years. The stuff I write is inspired by my life and all that's come with it, usual life stuff. Love, questions, death, travel, friendship, heartache, addiction, sunsets, loss, lemons, mental health, people, the outdoors, uncertainty, darkness and light, dreams, mistakes, and everything else.

Thank you to my family. Thank you to everyone who's encouraged and inspired me to write. Thank you to the friends who've told me to never stop writing, no matter what I'm feeling. Thank you to the friends who've encouraged me to share my thoughts, even when I'm afraid. Thank you to everyone who's put up with me and my crazy over the years, I'm forever thankful for your ears, hearts, and support. From the bottom of my heart, I am. And to one in particular, you know who you are - I would've been lost in life a thousand more times without you. Thank you so much for inspiring me in every way. Always have, always will.

Float The Day

Dreams Awake

Drop a line down through the clouds
and through the storms you'll catch the sounds.
You'll never be too far away,
we'll listen together every day.

You'll get down up in the sky,
laughter is our battle cry.
Swimming through five shades of blue,
you'll hear me here tomorrow too.

Our life becomes a song we wrote.
Every breath, a single note.
And we listen.
Dreams awake behind our eyes.

Fell down, fell back up again.
I can't recall just where I've been.
Listen to the things I hear,
and perfect places reappear.

Walking while words float around,
my shoes are where my feet are found.
I won a battle, stopped a war.
My dreams told me there's so much more.
'Imagine more.'

I close my eyes.
Upside down in the sky.
While dreams awake, we listen.

Thoughts From A Moon

What if truth is make believe?
There's so much curiosity.
What if the moon speaks to stars
and asks them how they're where they are?

How is it that I can be,
with all of this uncertainty?
How is it you got so far,
when I can't even find my car?

Why does distance never leave?
It seems to be surrounding me.
Why does evening make me glow?
Then I stand out and, I don't know...

Who would ever disagree
with dreams of fleeing to be free?
Who would wait and watch me grow
into myself before we go?

Sunshine sometimes feels like hell.
Tonight, I pray I'm my whole self.

Morning shows, I fade away
to hide behind another day.
When darkness comes, I'll find my way,
ignoring what the stars might say.
So much out there to think of.
So much out there to see.
As soon as stars stop watching,
I find that I am me.
As soon as stars stop watching,
I feel that I am free.

Morning Shows

Coat your throat.
Touch the sky.
Unroll the pool and float, so high.
Race on and on and you wanna slow down.

Days awake,
up so high.
Float on the pool, unroll the sky.
Way, way out there and you wanna come down.

To the ground you found eight months ago.

Seas of colors in bed, you know?
Coloring ceilings, morning shows.
I'd be asleep, but I never fall.
Just toss and turn, so I see it all.

Grab the mail,
small surprise.
Somehow four socks spark up two eyes,
few steps back and you wanna calm down.

Go to work,
rub your eyes.
Desert on socks, life's great surprise.
Way, way up there. When are you comin' down?

When you come down, come down.
Come down, take in this sky.

Storms Stumblin'

The sky cries when it needs to.
Wonder how long they've been falling.
Making their way way back up there,
just to fall again
when it all gets too heavy.

Storms stumble out to self reflection.
The distance finds its way to the dancing.
Thunder,
a little wonder, throwing beads down at the ground.

Wind wanders in to warm welcomes,
the feeling of never really leaving.
Knowing,
a little growing before the breeze rolls back around.

The wind blows when it's ready.
Wonder how long 'til we feel it.
Reeling it in, let it all go.
It comes back again
after it runs for a while.

Wind, don't think about the weather.
Storm, come stumblin' in.

Rooftop Stars

I'm up so high tonight,
so you can be by my side.
Watching the stars fall on down.
Staying this time around,
no one taught me how to land.

Sat on the moon tonight.
Back. You said, 'come in, don't hide.'
Brighter side you said you found,
ears heading to the ground,
no one taught me how to land.

I am a mountain, worthy climb.
I didn't build me up, but here I am.
Please don't build me up. Don't.
I'll only fracture it all.
Finally broke out to the outer ring,
a chance to sit on time's hands.
Take me to the coast of anything.
Edge of old and different.
Love, like gold, but different. Little harder.
Foam from sea on sand,
maybe that edge, I'll walk that line
between morning wake and always still.
Everything's gonna be fine.

My tail chasing me this time.

Rode on a star tonight.
Did you see me waving hi?
Crashed, then I burned, no doubt.
Wait for me if you come down,
no one taught me how to land.

Moved with the rain tonight
while you stayed up in the sky.
I wrecked myself on the ground,
catch me this time around,
no one taught me how to land.

That old rooftop, laughing at the town.
She was talking about time and space,
and how this life is not a race,
just before I woke up that morning.

Take me back to dreaming,
I'd be watching the stars fall down.
My tail chasing me this time.
Crashing into the ground.

Late Worm

All the birds were early.
Hanging, stalling in the sky.
Up, so high, so early.
They could see it in my eyes.

They learned to fly so early.
Bird's-eye judgement from above.
Up and down, so early,
before we find what we love.

We are the late worms.
Early birds don't matter.
Why worry about the time?
Get going when we're ready.

Early birds don't matter.

In my head I'm a lion.
I'm just lying in bed before I head for above.
I'm a late worm.
When I have legs I'll head for above.

With the wind they blindly sing.
They're early birds, we don't know anything.
We don't speak much.
We can't know a thing.
We don't sleep much,
so we see everything.

We don't sleep, so we see.
Early birds don't matter.
We are late worms, we don't care about the birds.
We don't sleep, so we see.

We hide underground. When it rains, we get too down.
Late worm's only early to a party that hasn't been planned.

Be By Now

Decisions, making tiny sense.
Unfailing, fallen - both sides of the fence.
Locked away, let it grow.
The further we go, the less we'll know.

Sipping coffee. Present tense.
Wonder where that memory went.
We stay young, we grow old.
We think so fast and move so slow.

I had no idea this is where I'd be right now.
I still don't know where I'll be by now.
Back from there and here somehow.

I don't know.

Drawing dishes, stop to think.
Satellites painting basements of sinks.
Sponges soaking, slowly grow.
Pillows deliver the day's final blow.

Tossing, turning, threw out tonight.
Beneath the bed, sea scorpions fight.
Never letting egos grow.
Habit. Leave a thank you as we go.

Sat in the sun.
Watched the rain
and I was so distracted.

Almost At Plaid

We saw the stardust echo late one Monday night.
You stood above my space ship, staring at the cabin lights.
Suddenly send the signal before we say farewell.
And all the doors are closing before you ring the bell.

We set out, the weather sets the pace.
Found out it snows out in outer space.
The stars spring at us, melting just before our eyes.
They always come back, it's just a matter of time.

There are lots of things that no one will ever know
and tonight we are going wherever we go.

Sometimes it seems not enough is too much.
So far, I've realized bizarre is now normal.

It didn't seem like enough.

They're shooting stars or wandering cars.
Windows rolled down, we rolled past your old town.
It was way out in the distance, where nothing is too far.

We'll have one of those weekdays.
Leave ourselves to find our place.
But, we'll pick up the pieces,
we'll never leave a trace.
Driving inside outer space.

Only Seen In Pictures

The pictures.
He's out there.
Creating waves.
You sat there.

He never understood it, he was a cool cat.
Enigma. There's something people dug about that.

He was always unaware, you knew he always knew.
Like all the times you said, 'I love you.'

They said he was gone.
I said 'I'll surprise you.'

I might lose it a lot, but my glass is never half empty.

Make my way through me as usual.

Where's the joy in not feeling free?
The way you smile in pictures
is the way you smile at me.

He's always on time and it's always too late.
Forget about time, have you not learned that I'll wait?

He goes to the same place a different way.
He goes somewhere out there where his road isn't paved.

They say he's out there.
Creating a way.
Saying, 'goodbye pictures' as he waves.
You sat there.

Headed Your Way

How is it sunny with so much rain?
What is creative? What is insane?

Why don't you smile? Where is your pain?
There's a light at the end of the tunnel and it's not a train.
I'm headed your way.

Star-lit lips, a hand on her hip.
She shoots, then blows on her two fingertips.
Never at me. As if I don't exist.

Day and night slide, the start of a trip.
She whispers, 'quiet' on one fingertip.
She looks toward me, but again we miss.

How is it sunny with so much rain?
What is creative? What is insane?

Why don't you smile? Where is your pain?
There's a light out there, and it's not a train.
I'm headed your way.

This city's skyline has shoulders.
She lives like she's never getting older.
A feeling so free, nothing could own her.

While memory lane gets colder,
I stroll through without ever getting older,
re-living all the secrets that I told her.

I aim for hearts and I always miss.
Today's the start of a life-long trip.
Feel free and settle down.

Static Screams From TVs

How do you spend your time?
Wake up children, play like the wind.

Why's my life a movie?
Why's my life a song?
I finally find the plot line and the characters are gone.
Silence when the soundtrack's wrong.

Why's my life a movie?
Why's my life a song?
I'm finally getting started, but the intro was too long.
Echoes where the peaks belong.

How do you spend your time?

Over in the corner life's record plays.
Needle rides the rails.
The line's not straight but it always follows anyway.

Songs skipped and they changed my days.
Wake up children, play like the wind.
How will you spend your time?

Static screams from TVs.

Whistle Humming

Sat on a suitcase, writing,
resembling different, winter weather biting.

Rode on a snowflake, painting,
assembling pigments, summer sunshine fainting.

The day, it leaves to find itself.
The night's just looking for answers.
Owls spin watching mermaids win,
while people pretend to know what they're doing.

We all catch up to us.
Just gotta let ourselves go.

Stood in a circus, stoking,
creating lifetimes, weekend wisdom joking.

Ran in a standstill, flying,
debating nice rhymes, season's cycle crying.

Chased life to the tracks, hands nailed to the ground.
Train whistle humming, under her sound.
She always shows up right on time.
Owls spin looking for answers.
Sunshine left us looking somewhere else.

In Your Radio

Ignore your light and dance in your darkness.
All that sunshine left a desert.
Remember, now was once never.

Follow your thunder and realize you're lightning.
The past adjusts your radio.
The songs that lead us where we go.

We strut through the storm as if it's just begun.

Nothing numb.
It's all real.
Where the hell is heaven?
What's that in your radio?
The sound of a silhouette
and a child's sunset when we're not young.

Songs leak from speakers, a sound about a star.
Evening. Before us, numbers glow.
Begin to feel and never know.

If you've never been lost, you will never be found.
We wake up here, disguise worn thin.
They'll never see just where we've been.

We strolled through the storm and onto the sun.

Splashing Underground

Purple lightning snapped above a desolate town.
She sang quiet's all I needed like she knew me.
Tilt my head up as I'm tailing down.
Closing my eyes as I splash through the ground.

Little dark and dirty down here.
Scary. Single little light spinning in the distance.
Think this thing's still floating.

Darkness breeds beauty, I suppose.
Balance, for me, the great unknown,
but I think I'm getting used to it.
Send a smile, a song,
a signal, what you're thinking.
No sinking.

She flipped and fell
into a hole that only a star would stumble upon.
I wrote my thoughts out years before I had them.

Living life in the wake, watching over.
Saw a sailboat sitting in the stars the other evening.
What if everything matters?
Lighthouse, lonely, but saving some days.
Fragile, still standing to help them find our way.

Orchids grew right on the sky Thursday night.
Maybe she knew we were watching.
Spinning in the distance,
to help us find our way.

Leaving Left Field

Towels, walking sand.
The sun rolled down.
Mountains will tell you it melted the ground.

She walked out from left field.
She sang by my side,
and she suddenly realized
that we can make our own time.
Tied it all up, that's a wrap.
Into the heart of a new scene.

Every great falls before greatness.
No laughs without aching.
That's when she left left field.

It was dark, it was evening.
Sunshine smashed on down.
It was parked illegally,
well beyond this worn out town.

We all left with the evening.
Rainbows rode on clowns.
Carousel parachutes fell
into reflections on the sound.

We were with the evening.
Left field, we were leaving.

Hear You Sing

Rainbows on sidewalks, imitating crows.
Insane goes inside, walks in to where we go.
It's not his say, so we can breathe.
At the end of the day, I just wanna hear you sing.

We never care when we feel surrounded,
time always finds its way around it.
You'll be with me on cloud nineteen
at the end of someday when I hear you sing.

From the window, moving mountains.
I think of it all.
We were younger. We were crazy.
We were having a ball.

We pull our hoods up in the rain.
We get older, memory frays.
This same spot, sitting here, you sang.
But, that was yesterday.

Clouds sit and stare at empty parking lots a lot.
Watching people walking out, they forgot.
They just watch. Watch and let them be.
They know tonight they're gonna hear you sing.

Plant seeds on cement, cities never slow.
Never taking time, complaining nothing grows.
I'd give you my time if I knew it would mean
at the end of the day I'd get to hear you sing.

Somehow Have Me

Skipped stones and steeped thought.
I walked for years before I got lost.
And I never knew I'd be alright
if I slept all the way through the night.

There is a light inside me.
It gets so bright, it blinds me.
We speak through song
and I don't know what I'm sending.
Just like how it sounds.

I didn't know what I was sending,
now I'm singing in my head.
These songs, they whisper
while I'm laying in my bed.

There is a spark inside me.
It breaks the dark, it starts me.
We speak through song
and I can feel what you're sending.
I always like how it sounds.

You seem to know what you're sending.
Like your heart heard what was said.
Your songs, somehow, have me
feeling home in my own bed.

Your songs, somehow, have me.

Only your songs.
Have me home in my own bed.
Send me your song.
Send me to sleep.
There are dreams in my head.

Your songs, somehow, have me
feeling home in my own head.

Perfect On A Rooftop

Call me from a rooftop.
I sit down below.
Slanted little rooftop.
Just to say hello.

Call me when the day's done.
Talking with your fears.
After speaking, day's done.
You'll go over there.

Do we balance one another?
Are we equally off tilt?
We make me be better.
I hope that this won't be.
When everything just feels better,
but it's not near me.

Give me a call to talk.
Give me a talk to breathe.
Give me a call to talk at night.
Talk until I sleep.

Calming on a rooftop.
I just watch the sky.
Perfect on a rooftop,
feelings in her eyes.

Call me when I'm painting.
You send me the song.
I am only painting
so you can write along.

Call me from a rooftop.
Give me a talk to breathe.
I would meet you anywhere.
Talk so I can sleep.

Speak

I drive west when I don’t know what to do.
I fall in love and I don’t know why.
Our feet heading east ‘cause the weather won’t change.
You’re by my side,
toes on the dash.
Decembers together.

Now I’m thinking.
I’m not talking.
I stop thinking
when I’m talking.
Can’t stop thinking.

I’m up, I’m down.
I’m up, I’m down.
I said too much.
You’re not around.

You do best when I don’t know what to do.
I lose control and I don’t know why.
I’m the only one I’ve talked to for two days.
It's all outside.
Frames on the wall.
Remember together.

Speak to me so I won’t think.

Silent Space

Where am I going?
What do I do?
It would all be easier if I could still ask you.

What am I doing?
You disappeared.
These days I wish that you were still here.

Silent space to ponder.
All the ones who got away.
Your favorite people's final days.
All the things you didn't say.
All the reasons people pray.
I'll just listen.

Why do I wake up?
The less I know, the more it all means.
When will I wake up?
Beginning and end, but what's in between?

Where am I going?
What should I do?
This would all be easier if I could still ask you.

I never lied, because I never knew.

I still speak to you
and I just listen.

Clown Shoe Blues

Do you know where your stairway goes?
Will you be happy off your throne?
Leaving everything you've ever known?
Do you realize you're not alone?

Was it your decision?
The colors and the work and the vision.
Are you gonna miss it?
Dismiss it?
How will you know if you don't go?
In the middle, you're in it.
How will you live if you don't grow?
How do you find decisions anyway?

Some might say, 'wise beyond your years.'
Some might say, 'buried by your fears.'
Thinking comes as creative disappears.
They have no idea just what he hears.
'My favorite, a genius, so quiet,
do more, do this, like him, make it fade.
One of a kind, you'll be nothing.'
Close my eyes 'til they go away.

Time will tell where these shoes will go.
Never cared if I'm on my own.
Moments seized outweigh weekends blown.
Everybody loves him, still he stands alone.

Will you be happy when you're free?
'Why are people amazed by me?
Maybe they see me differently.'
Stare at my shoes,
What should I be?

Break Inside, Building

I am not a writer.
I am not a light.
I am just a little thought
moving with the night.

I am not a circus.
I am not a clown.
I am a half-balanced act,
one foot on the ground.

I don't know where I'm going,
don't even know where I've been.
Somewhere, well before the beginning,
or a few feet past the end.

I'll follow you if you'll follow me.
Help me follow me.

I am no director.
I won't cut this scene.
This is when we break inside,
building who we'll be.

I am not a rocket.
I am not a cloud.
I am just a falling star,
drifting without sound.

I don't know where I'm going,
don't even know where I've been.
Take me, well before the beginning,
or a few feet past the end.

I gotta follow me. I'm following.
Soul spread thin.
I gotta spread my soul so thin.
I gotta get around time's corner.
I gotta wait, I need a win.
I stopped these to see if I was me.
Just wanna get around this corner.

Center Of Gravity

He's no genius, enigma, just fix it, he thinks.
He says, 'I think, maybe, they don't think enough.
Maybe, don't feel enough.
Always have, always will was said.
Maybe just a little different
and there's always music in the background.

There's just so much out there.
So many people out there.
So many things to see.
They've seen it the whole time and
I've never known what's happening,
so where is my center of gravity?

People you have wrapped around your finger,
drown them out like rings down drains.
Where'd we leave those things?
Is it just me, or has everybody else gone insane?
How do they not see
what's going to be happening?

I think they wound up writing a book about it,
but he built a cabinet and croaked
on a mountain near a desert, something like that.
Then a buncha people believed him.
I don't know, didn't read it.
What if this is our last dinner?
Be sure to pile your plate. Take a second, helping.
Serve it up. Breathing.
Nobody believes me.

People lose their minds sometimes.
I never lose it, just leave it.
Just gotta leave some things sometimes,
come back when you're ready.'

But, that was just him talking.
He never knew what he was talking about.
They never knew what he was thinking about.
He never knew what was happening,
and he found no use in a center of gravity.

He said, 'gravity seems to walk on me.'

Two Piece Puzzle

He's an idiot genius.
He's a tortured heart.
He's a one piece puzzle
that somehow falls apart.

He's spinning vinyl's brainchild.
He's so goddamn smart.
He's a two piece puzzle
that no one ever starts.

His life is these pieces, hers is all the art.
Fill in all of these pieces.
Every morning, end of every night,
fill up cups, glasses, creases.
A flight or a day away.

He says life is wandering.
He says it will be great.
He's a dusty puzzle
that tries not to complain.

He's a nightmare's nightmare.
He is just a dream.
He's a scattered puzzle
that no one's ever seen.

He's not make believe.
Leaves under the blood red moon.
Into these pieces leaks, you.

What He's Doing

They say he's right all the time, it's his art.
They say he writes all the time, must be smart.
He says,
Right.
I don't know what I'm doing,
I'm just doing, I'm lost, I'm doing.
I'm just looking, not lost, I'm thinking.
I know there's more.
It's not right, this part.
He says he's not right all the time, it's just art.
Says, I don't write all the time, it's my heart.
He's broke, a joker, can't play poker and he knows
Nothing.
One thing.
Maybe
There's no right.
There's no right way for anything.
Wait for the right day and fly away.
Some day. They say
It's all right in front of you.
You won't miss flights if you learn to fly.
Heart's handwriting gets handed down.
I was gonna fly.
I know you'll fly.
He's so smart, he's right.
It's just art, he writes.
Heart, he writes.
It's nothing.
What I'm doing.

In His World

From another place or from another time,
he drove outside to take a stroll in his mind.

Makes up he's a fire,
tells him it's just rain.
Soon, he says, the light comes back.
In his world where there's no pain.

Makes up he's a memory.
Tells him he's in style.
Soon, he says, it's belly laughs.
In his world where it's all smiles.

Makes up he's an old worm.
Tells him she's above.
Soon, he says, you'll find your beak.
In his world where it's all love.

Makes up he's a sidewalk.
Tells him it just weaves.
Soon, he says, it circles back.
In his world where no one leaves.

Brings it all, any time life brings it.
Mind never makes up for anything.
Soul only ever brought anything.
And in his own little world, that means everything.

Road To Myself

Now I can speak.
Now I can feel.
Now I can see that this is all real.

I want to sleep.
I want to fly.
I want to be more than just a guy.

I'm writing in traffic.

Meandering car alarms and people crossing.
Nobody knows where they're going.
That's why we sit. Going.
No cause for alarm.
Out of sight, on my mind.
This road isn't easy, but it'll all be worth it.

Look at my smile.
Look at me now.
Look out and see that I made it somehow.

My road to myself.
My road to the road.
My road to all that I'm yet to know.

I was just thinking in traffic.

Zebra's Plea

I leave on a crosswalk
hidden in the trees.
Bark is black and white
so they won't see me.

Hide me on a mountain.
Hide my rosy cheeks.
I'll be up so high
that they don't see me.

Black and white, not hiding.
Words, like me, move gently.
Timelines lie.
We live a little differently.
Patiently.

My lines aren't straight.
My nights are days.
It's up or down or black or white.
No in between today.
I'd be just fine if I could
find myself a little gray.

Need to get a little gray.

I jump in an old frame.
Kicking by the sea.
Photos, black and white
so they don't see me.

Hide me in the paper.
Hide me - A,B,C.
Crosswords, black and white.
They'll never see me.

My lines aren't straight.
My nights are days lying gently.
Patiently.

Give me a little gray.
Please, give me a little gray.
Today.

Like A Loris

My train goes uphill.
My train seeking thrill.
My train, slowly like a loris.
My train always will.

My plane goes upstairs.
My plane, bending air.
My plane, hanging like a loris.
My plane way up there.

I was waiting.
Watching the sky, signs flicker 'on time.'
Wondering which one was you.
Waiting. Watching.
I picked up when you came down
for a few days before goodbyes.

No sleep tonight, you've got to fly.
You know right where my door is.
Grilling time and killing flies
before you leave me like a loris.

My time leaves today.
My time never stays.
My time flitting like a loris.
My time goes away.

My day spent outside.
My day in my mind.
My day loving like a loris.
My day by your side.

I picked up when you came down
for a few nights before goodbyes.

Favorite Road

Sat out in the sun and thought of a drive.
The one we'll take when I'm with you.
Smile at me like the ocean smiles.
We'll find our favorite road.

The key to my home is inside your home
and I watch the sky crawl by.
I said I'd call, but I meant please call me.
Hear what you want, spread your wings and fly.

Let me in so I can watch myself in the past from above.
I don't know. No one knows where I'll go.
They think I'm a genius and I'm locked out.
I know exactly where I went, but I don't know where I'll go.

Walked into the sun and thought of that drive,
I guess I had nothing better to do.
You smiled at me, and patiently
we found our favorite road.

We don't know where it goes.
It's not where we went, it's where we'll go.
We'll go see where it goes.

Tell Stories

Listening to raindrops.
Look up to the sun as they stop.
You start to speak as we roll to the top.

While windows skim,
the wind comes in.
And out of your mouth,
the story you told me about
lonely mermaids in the snow.
Frozen there, while winter glares
until the sun walks in.
Ice softens, flakes meet water.
Sheds some skin.
She re-begins.
She learns to swim again.

Tell stories, I'll listen.
Roll up the windows and listen.
Late at night I listen.
I look and I listen.
I'm up. Like windows, I listen.

Our terrain changes
like we're on another planet.
Like it was how we've always planned it.

Mermaids moving a movie.
We begin.
Like characters after the credits end.

Own Way Home

A young man's out looking for a new town,
looking for an old sound.
He's been looking for a place
where there aren't too many people around.

In an old town where nobody knows his name.
Oblivious to fame.

He's dreaming of warmer weather,
stringing stars together
and making his own way home.

She's been searching for a sane place,
dancing with her own grace.
She's been searching for a town
where she'll never ever have to hide her face.

A peaceful place where nobody's seen her crown.
It'll never get found.

So, she dreams of calm forever,
stringing stars together
and making her own way home.

Their lines intertwine while arranging the sky.

Create some calmer weather.
Stringing stars, together.
Evening floats like feathers
and they make their own way home.

A little look.
A little trust and a smile.

Evening Weeks

Storyteller, find your voice,
turn these pages to a choice.
They're stuck in hell without a sail,
so please return and spill your tale.

Life contestant, choose a door.
Your two options: change or more.
You can't come back if you don't leave.
Are you afraid of what you need?

Shaking frames, easel breathing.
Enough of everything, release me.

Whisper to night,
mind conversations walk up to the mic.
Colors leak into black and white,
and words are finally speaking.

Writer, writer, write it out.
Make sense of nothing with no doubt.
If you stay here you'll never know
what will happen if you go.

Painter, painting, make it loud.
Wear your colors and be a clown.
Every brushstroke is a day,
can't fathom why you'd still use gray.

Black and white suddenly speaking.
Black and white colored in, breathing.
Finally speaking with evening,
with words, somehow, bringing us life.

Comfortable

It's flesh in front of black and white.
The one you think of every night.
The sting of a spring, floating away.
The one with whom you know you're safe.
So you make yourself comfortable.

Morning, lift you through the window.
Locked it all up and forgot the code.
Sleeping, cabins, dream next to you.
Sunday, drinking the life that we've brewed.
One day we will be comfortable.

I'll warm up the engine and we'll go.
Somewhere, anywhere, I don't know.
Sing old songs next to me at night.
'I know I caught your eye.'
Blood moonlight, morning drive.

It's heart in front of shine and gold.
The ones you're with as you grow old.
You've always seemed to know the way.
We'll mark the 'X' and bury the safe,
then we'll make ourselves comfortable.

Puzzle pieces, together, apart.
Together, alone, it's just the start.
Dreaming of those chairs on a beach
with all the lessons time will teach,
and we will be so comfortable.

We miss signs and somehow make it.
State line, moonlight, morning drive.

Life In A Day

A lifetime is a day.
Each evening is a breath.
Did you waste any sunsets?
Did you get enough rest?

Each city is a stoplight.
Every risk, a step.
Each postcard is a letter,
or a promise that you kept.

Who did you spend your time with?
How did you spend your day?
Did you do everything you wanted?
Did you say what you wanted to say?

Tell me,
how was today?

Angels meet angels. It's art,
emotion, a new tattoo.
Whenever you're feeling lost,
just a stop to tie your shoe.

A bad year, a bruise.
A song, a single note.
Were you happy with your breakfast?
Did you get some peace and float?

Did you make the most of your afternoon?
Smaller people's mornings too?
You know, the stars could shine through very soon.

Hear It In The Writing

Wherever you are tonight,
I hope you're happy.
Hope you're filled.
If you're not, just come my way.
I've got so much, I spill.

Overflowing with love.
Overflowing with things I never could get enough of.
Like it was there all along,
I just heard the same songs differently.
Suppose I listen differently.
Learn a little differently.

Shine, please.
You know I know what's in you.
Shine, please.
When you do, it's all I see,
and there's too much left here to leave.

Whatever you're doing tonight,
I hope you're smiling.
That wherever you are, you're good.
If you're not, just come my way,
we'll figure out what could.

Live wild, and so patiently.
Learned I learn things differently,
I let me get the best of me,
when I hide inside the rest of me.
Whatever you're doing tonight.

Almost To Packing

What if I said there's no ego?
If I said it's only pride.
What if you knew what I've been through?
Would you run away and hide?

What if I said I'm just nervous?
If I said that and I'm shy.
What if you thought I was judging?
Your mind can tell you big lies.

No better or judgement,
Just nervous, thinking or thrilled.
I know where I've been.
I deserve a win.
But, until then,
I'll keep trying to figure out
how I know how this all works.

It'll take me 30 years
to tell you where the last 30 years took me.
I've still got so much time.

What if you said I'm a lost cause?
If you told them I was done.
What if they weren't really finished
when they all said they had won?

What if you said I'm a bad guy?
If you said I didn't care.
What if I came down from heaven,
to make people like you scared?

Every single person walking by
has their own crazy, different, life.
Do you ever realize you have no idea?
Why don't they stop to talk about it?

Absence Of Nothing

In the absence of nothing.
With the exception of everything.
We will all find that our memories mean anything.
What does this mean to you?

Overdriven and going nowhere.
Knowing where I've been.
Is it harder to change or stay the same?

Push me past forty.
I'm already over the hill.

My favorite piece of earth has grown.
The only peace of mind I've known.
Broken brick, window to my back.
The sky, blue, chimes for my eyes.
I could hear it.

It means exactly nothing.
You say that you've got everything.
Soon you will find that gold can be anything.
What does this mean for you?

You're driving over nowhere.
This place has spring in winter.
What did that mean to you?

Bring A Mountain

He's not afraid, he's just had a long day.
At times, he feels he knows he's losing it.
He's not losing it, but it's not next to him.
Reuses shedded skin. Worn thin,
his mind's in a million places.
Sleeplessness sleeps in the lines on his face
and New York won't stop writing letters.

The strings in the ears she gave him were singing.
Tonight.
Just come down, bring a mountain.
Come down, bring a smile.
Hey. Come down, bring a memory.
Come down for more than a while.

For more than a while, he wrote.

He's still awake, because he had a long day.
Last night, the time he wrote he's tired of it.
He's not tired of it, but it scrambles him.
Knees bruised and shredded fins, he swims
through time instead of leaving traces.
Restlessness wrecks all these moments and grace
and Tucson won't stop calling today.

His anchor, she's away. Way out on a mountain.
She built the hammer she builds her home with.
She swims in the sea.
He built his life with the life he'd been building.
He walks tired, but free.
Days awake, anchor's far away.
Funny how a memory can
ring you up, and walk right in
and change your day.

Drinking Names

By a lake, familiar songs behind me.
Leaves, like school busses, climb fire up the siding.
Does anyone ever notice?

They sit and stand on still water,
wind slides, winds between them.
Rock stacked tower, twelve inches on the surface.
Do they ever even notice?

She hides at a hotel, she's drinking her name.
He stands there and watches the impending fame.
She grinds, she's her own boss,
there's no one the same.
He's been here, he's waiting, his life is his game.

The sky's so blue and I'm down here, so high.
Do you ever smile just to get by?

She'll live in the ocean, she'll go get some sun.
He'll sleep in his own bed when the day is done.
She'll throw her arms around him
when the morning comes.
He'll listen to her soft eyes and never have to run.

With a little time, I think. I think with too much time.
So I just started spinning.
We are all just spinning.

Denver To The Desert

The leaves changed with the terrain.
Leaves left and came with the terrain.
We listened to the Cities during sunset here.
Years ago.
So, I gave it a spin in the dark.
Thought of you and then everything.

Her crazy drives me wild
Her insane makes me smile.
Maybe she just amazes me.
It's been forever since anything has.
Will you wait for me?

Right now, to me, love means everything.
The weight of waiting.
Find peace in creating.
What does what you do mean to you?
What does it bring to you?
What means what love means?
Nothing.
It feels like everything.
What means more than what love means?
Nothing. It's everything.

Paul and June were singing songs about waiting.
The day was fading.
Tom was breaking, but it's alright.
Tires weren't moving, I was tired.
Fading. Feeling crazy.
Let's go.

Crazy.
Make me question me and then learn.
A lesson with myself without a chalkboard.
Relax, water, and breathe.
Hope I get to me in time for you.

Leaves left hours ago, I did too.
All these things we'll overcome
Before we find we've just begun.
In my head, I'm already in bed
and I'm not alone.
We've had so many beginnings.
I could have sworn I took this turn already.
In my head, I'm already in bed,
and I know I'm not alone.

Sleep Driving

You talk about early, but you've never met late.
Do you ever wonder why some people stay?

You think about dreaming, but don't get a taste.
Do you ever wonder why some people wait?

Eat when you're hungry, breathe when you're lost.
Remember those nights and all that you've got.
Do you think it's chance you made it?

You wave when I'm walking
and your eyes set my pace.
Do you ever rewind and still win the race?

You know when I'm trailing
and you show me your grace.
Do you ever rewind just to see a face?

Let it go to waste. You won't get a taste.
I can't see the two faces who know me.
I don't ever run, I just win the race.
My head's so far ahead it's trailing.
Let's get together. Let's not think about dreaming.

Television Glow

You shine.
You're dark.
I love the way you shake.

You're fine.
You're smart.
I love the way you make it.

I didn't mean to leave us.
I didn't mean to slide.
I don't know why I push me off
when we're still on the ride.

Your shine.
Your dark.
I love the way you fake it.

Your line.
Your heart.
Nothing will ever break it.

You lie.
Your art is something the world's never seen.
Arrive.
The start is right where you've always been.
The world will never see it,
'cause I won't let me be.

They will never see it,
so it will always be.

Coffee Stained Sunset

She's the blinds which I turn
day and night, altering it all.

She's the kite that I fly
wind will bite, but never break this line.

I understand it all, I really do.
Time's a doorway I lean on,
just holding it open for you.

This warm desert winter,
sunshine shows up and leaves
to come back around again.
I'm looking up to the sky.

She's the coffee I drink,
nice and cold, I think, I want it all.

She's the leaves on the trees,
they will fall, but they'll land right on me.

Always land right on me.
Understand, I really do.
Pushes and pulls, the wind it bends,
I hold on tight to my best friends.

Float The Day

Plan the week, how to hide.
Float on the pool or live inside.
Call you up, hear you smile.
I'll be right there in 14 miles.

Roll out west, have some fun.
We loved that song when we were young.
I'm not me. You're not you.
When far away, it's always true.

Call me when you're clean and we'll start a new day.
We wash away our yesterdays and start over any time.

Follow my heart.
Follow your soul.
Live each day and I'll never get old.

Show up late, float the day.
I'm sinking up, please go away.
Being lost got me here,
but somehow, now, life's crystal clear.

My best friend by my side.
Comfortable, like I've arrived.
We wake up, find ourselves.
Without ourselves there's nothing else.

Follow your heart.
Follow my soul.
Live each day and you'll never get old.

Broken Wing

I fall into a hole in the sky.
Swimming with stars
before I wash up on shore.

Broken wing, won't fly anymore.

Started strutting across the sand.
Passing castles
and shovels, seeking out your door.

Broken wing, won't fly anymore.

I need another bird with a broken wing
to sing and strut through life with me.

Stood on the corner of your street.
Birds-eye, window.
I saw you pecking at the floor.

Broken wing, won't fly anymore.

I fell for you on fallen wires.
You caught me walking,
so we walked a little bit more.

Broken wing, don't need to fly anymore.

We walk,
strut, dance,
talk
a little more.
We don't need to fly anymore.

Broken wing,
sing and strut through life with me.

To The Nest

To the beach, to the party,
to the nest after starting.

With our feet, with our feathers,
with our storms, to calmer weather.

Two birds stroll against sand,
pecking through trash and scanning the land.
Convinced with time they'll soar like lemons,
in time, they'll float to old hands.

Flip the sky, flip the sunset.
Flip the deck, have we won yet?

Dive to sea, dive to borders.
Dive through time, try to warn her.

Out walking again, these wings, we won't need them.
We'll be running.
With nothing again, these things, we don't need them.
We'll be breathing.

Get Me There

We just pulled over here for a moment.
We lay with our backs in the grass.
Poking holes in the sky, we're staring through the night.

We're not the same as you and me.
All I do is wonder what to do.
Occasionally, I think of you.
The thought of you can change my day.
Get me there when I lose my way.

A partner in crime when your life's on the line.
Pulled over for a moment.

We lay with our backs in the grass.
Poking holes in the sky, we're staring through the night.

The only sound - the stars passing by cars.
Passed people are peepholes in the sky
at night and they're not that far.

Stars were holes in the sky.
We were staring through the night.

They're not that far if we can see their light.

Back in the grass. no sounds, no sights.
We close our eyes and we say goodnight.

We pulled over here just for a moment.

Beyond Between

We fell into my car.
We spilled into the stars.
We understood half of what we'd heard so far.

We went out beyond the town.
We walk out when we can't stand to sit down.
We went out beyond where we'd ever been found.

We lived between the nights.
With love between our lies.
We saw right through them with our own four eyes.

Wind whispered through window cracks.
The radio singing, driving down our backs.
We didn't say anything.
Just listening.

We didn't make it, but close.
We lost our way when we left the coast.
Nothing's ever enough these days, not even the most.

We brought all the thoughts that we knew.
We were on the verge of breaking through.
We misplaced the memory of what we came here to do.

We spilled out of my car.
We fell into the stars.
We didn't understand what we'd done so far.

Wait Forever

I blasted off.
I got a little lost.
I came back down after it all came out.

I took time off.
We got a little lost.
Under the moon there's a little more room.

The dark days we once knew.
The shadows that you wore.
The reasons that we grew.
The words that you once wove.
I'll wait forever to grow old with you.

The day wears off.
Maybe the sun gets lost.
We don't need its rays. We light a fire. We stay.

Shadows take off.
Moving as water, lost.
Using you as the palette on which they draw.

Shadowed like they've always known you.
I'll wait forever to grow old with you.

Forget Footprints

One evening, a moon lit up oceans of snow,
revealing a highway where four soles would go.

Time piecing tiles for water to fall on.
Pictures, picture perfect. I fell right in.
Like lemons on a birthday, a trophy from a friend.

Never stopped to learn
how to say what should be said
to help me remain unknown,
and two show up as soon as the other two go.
Show me your scars and I'll trust you,
twirl and paint you brighter blues.

Light, piecing pigments for happy to nap on.
Pixels, picture perfect. I fell right in.
Like laughter on a birthday, a letter from a friend.

This evening, we stumbled up to our dreams.
These mirrors, showing footprints
where four feet had been.

Something's so different. So much. The same.
Two went left right there,
two just disappeared.
Time out for finding, time out for flying.
Calm down, you're flying.
Come down, you're fine.
Pushing through, leaving time tapering
as though the past had never begun.

We walked, talking on the sand,
never looking back.
We stumbled into our dreams.
Tomorrow sings a little louder,
brighter shade of you.

Down To Build It

Hurricane mermaid, felt you coming.
Steady, slowed, and ready to steal me away.
I saw it, I saw it all, I saw everything in that night.
Shore, shore, it's fine, saw it all.
The storm that swam underneath the marquee.

Carefree worrier, cautious warrior
reconvening one day under sunshine.
Hurricane mermaid saw it all coming.
Never stay, can't leave, anyway. Never running.
Keep swimming
while we cultivate our own gardens,
reconvening when they're ready.

After it storms for a while,
a little sunshine's bound to breakthrough.

Maybe change our names and replant this thing.
Floating so long, losing roots.
Dropped off in the desert.
Water and sunshine myself.
Swear I've been through this before.
The brightest flowers seem to sink
before blooming again.
The way love stumbles through life,
rumbling through this garden.
Petals push themselves,
coloring hills, hues of future and familiar.
Always understanding
what sleeps inside of a storm.

Hurricane come back again.
Tear a house down to build it.
Hurricane, won't you be my friend?
Wash away whatever with time
and watch as it begins.
Wash away whatever with time.

Little Love Lean

I believe the brighter the light,
the darker the demons.
Man, I'm like a moth.
Take me to the evening.

There's always been something about it,
been loving that light forever.
Deep love without demons doesn't exist.
Demons leave and leave it room to live.
Everybody's got a skeleton somewhere.
Been desperate for dark forever,
there's always been something about it.

I believe the darker the night,
the later I'm leaving.
Man, I'm like a moth.
Get me through the evening.

Light creaks in as a little door opens.
Done-with demons flee, too tired to fight.
I see a little love lean in.
Oh what a beautiful evening,
back in the grass, taking off for dark and light.

Dust from stars, like morning moths.
Star, stay there 'til I get there.
A little too lost in the darkness.
A little too close to the light.

Easy Intrigue

Chase a ball on a field,
spin old earth on a wheel.
You'll be like your idols,
all your fallen idols.

Write a book, make it real.
Your ideas that people steal.
They'll be like your idols,
They'll never get to idle,
they won't have the key.

It's everything I've ever done.
It's everything that I'll do next.
It's everything I would have won.
It's everything's easy.

And I don't forget.

Lifetimes ago I told you that I'm never done.
It's never enough.
Can't create enough.
Cleanse my palette,
scrape it up real rough.
Moving on's not giving up.

I think back.
I don't look back.
Maybe I went back?
Slow me down.
Fast forward, now
I think I'll slow me down.
Just for a minute.
Get me back on track.
I think.
Back.

Nothing's not easy.
Please, please appease me.
Please, something intrigue me.
Please don't make it easy,
or I'm worried I will leave it.

Nothing comes naturally.
It's all so natural, you see?
It all feels like nothing,
The day-to-day to me.
My nothing's the stuff of dreams.
But, dreams aren't what I want to be.

It's not easy if I think about it.

Can't do if I think about it.

Fixing Buttons

I couldn't stop and I couldn't go.
Time is nothing but more, or less, time.
And what if it ends tomorrow?

We never know what we're gonna be,
but we can be more than what we can see.

What's obvious to others, I don't heed.
'Til I topple down to find me in me,
eventually.

If I drop this, what else will I not need?
How's it been so long that I couldn't see?
Up and down, then crawl and climb.
Elevators drop a step sometimes.

Things are bound to happen, no reason or rhyme.
My roof caved in and I thought I was fine.
Trapped in the air and I couldn't just be.
No parachute, down. Yet, somehow, you caught me.

I couldn't stop and I couldn't go.
It was right there and I didn't know.
Fixing buttons day and night,
One step down before I rise.

Once The Captain

I was once the sand
carrying the sea,
and every sleepless night
they walked all over me.

I was once the colors
reflected by the sea.
I was so magnificent.
They always looked at me.
They walked all over me.

So, tonight I'm stepping out.
Stepping out past me.
Tonight I'm stepping out
to see what I will be.

Out past the edge, that's where I'll be.
Out past the edge is where you'll find me.

I was once the captain,
the captain of the sea.
They thought because I laughed,
I didn't take it seriously.

I was once the letters,
handwritten by the sea.
Now that they've found power,
they've forgotten about me.
They have no use for me.

I was once the captain,
carrying the sea,
reflecting all the colors,
laughing seriously.
I was once the captain.

Bowman's Log

Leave us where we left off.
Leave from where we started.
Steady this ship with wild, selfless wind.

Take us where we're ready.
Take, from us, that thinking.
Secure this sail with warm, reckless wind.

The sun was setting in the center of the road.
Slept in Now, where there's no unfamiliar.
Songs soar beneath, singing out my day.
No concern for where we're going,
knowing we're on our way.
Where there's no unfamiliar.

Time's tide taking us.
Dark's light rising, right between two yellow lines.
Write before we float ashore.
Oh, captain, captain, call to me.
So far out here, can't you see?
This far gone's not make believe.
Oh captain, captain, call to me.

Bring us words we left out.
Bring this, we are ready.
Balance this barque with far less wind.

Find us time to wander.
Find out what we've needed.
Balance this boat with a cool west wind.

The sun was setting in the center of the road.
Oh, captain, captain, call to me.

Diving Board

I walked across my brain today
while I was crossing the street.
I walked outside the lines today,
they watched me from the back seat.

I talked about the day today
while I was stacking ice cream.
I talk and don't know what I say.
I taught me all that I'll need.

Sometimes I set sail to see,
see what I'm gonna be.

Make this plank a diving board
and then I'll learn to swim.
Untie my mind and have some more,
tomorrow I'll begin.

I walk out to sea.
I wade endlessly.
At least that's how it seems.
Lose my feet,
I'll blend in with the stars.

I built a rocketship today
while it was raining outside.
Old quilt and cushions, fly away
out past everything I've ever tried.

I spent a lot of myself today,
Then I went flying alone.
When I let go in outer space,
somehow I feel like I'm home.

Hold your breath in outer space.
Somehow I feel like I'm home.
Yeah, I'll blend in with the stars.

Drip Castle

He'd run until he ran out of land,
thinking, 'maybe find me a mermaid.'
What he'd let slip away,
dripping through his hand
above the beach, down into a castle.

Sitting on the sand, eight feet east of the coastline.
Why do I stare at the crashing?
Why do I wander at night?
Why do I believe that these waves are listening?

Glimmer on the ocean, moon deflecting light.
Twinkle in the distance, the sparkle in her eyes.

As bright as the stars, and as out there as ever.

She'd go until she'd gone twice around,
singing, 'come on, find me a calm shore.'
What she'd once hoped, for more,
swashing through her hands
beneath the beach, up into a castle.

Staring at the sand, little ways west of the coastline.
Why do I live in the crashing?
Why do I call out at night?
Why do I believe that those flames are listening?

Flicker on the foam's edge, crackling little coal.
A fire where the tide ends, the warmth inside his soul.

As bright as the stars, and as out there as ever.

Others say it's burned-out.
Others say she's out there.

Bring The Ocean

Rippling, crashing like clouds to the ground.
Doesn't recall if he really said that out loud.
Patience, like praying for a tide's return.
Doesn't recall if he really said that to her.
Come on, bring the ocean.

The wind blows blues out of order.
Tell him he's crazy, he adores her.
She's a tidal wave, changing it all out at sea.
Building up love, to demolish me.

Tumbling, softly like thoughts against wind.
Doesn't recall if she really said that to him.
Loyal, like evening at the end of the day.
Doesn't recall if she really said it that way.
Come on, bring the ocean.

The wave moves moods, a blue sky swims.
Tell her she's lost it, no one's like him.
He's a cycling storm, drafting out soul in the breeze.
Stirring up love, to overwhelm me.

Soulful little bird singing on a shoulder
sings come back, sings come back, sings come back.
Sings won't you listen to me?
Young man, tired, out standing on a beach.
Wind and waves like ocean and sand.
He doesn't say a thing.
Thinks,
come on, demolish me.

Fleets Of Thought

From my mountain I survey the sea.
Always the one questioning,
what do people think of me?

Waves of watered down people
walking beneath.
I don't think they'll ever see
that they're half of who they used to be.

Hidden by a cloud,
they come to me in fleets.
I come to me and leave.

My youth's fountain pushes me
toward the parts of me to be,
the parts to leave,
and everything I think I'll need
to get me through today.

Waves of little lost people
lying beneath.
I don't think they'll ever see
that they're who they said they'd never be.

Silence screams out loud.
They come to me in fleets.
I come to me and leave
to get me through the day.

I'll Be The Sand

Untied the tangle up here to spill a few thoughts
about thinking, love, and living.
Though, I'm not certain I really know a thing.
Like, you'd be a queen, but I'll never be a king.

So, we've got imagination.

I'll be the sand, ready to play.
You'll be the wind, you'll blow me away.

I'll be the sunset, you'll be the wake.
You'll wander, roving, while my mirror shakes.

I'll be the moon and you'll be a star,
and I'll come and go, while you shine so hard.

You'll be the ocean and I'll be the sand,
and you'll pummel me and I'll understand.

I'll be the sand. I understand.
Show up, blow me away.

So, we've got imagination
and footprints by the sea.
You'd be a queen,
but I don't think I'll ever be a king.
Seems life is living, love, and thinking.
I'll be the sand.
Please. Show up, blow me away.

Why Wait Now?

Opportunity sleeps in the center of struggle.
It's time to wake up.

Wake up.
Up there.
They're here.
Hear waves.
Wake up.

Stretch all four in the morning and you come alive,
like words as music surrounds them.

Joy scatters grief. Drowning false while fulfilling true.
That's when you wake up.

Wake up.
Up there.
They're here.
Hear waves.
Wake up.

Stretch all four in the morning and you come alive,
like words as music surrounds them.

Do you remember what the future told you?
You were a child by the ocean.
Hand-built castles in the sand, you played.
Rewind faster past the land they paved,
before it goes away.

Weather And A Woman

Where is my ship?
Who moved my shit?
Been sleeping nine to five.
Seems something isn't right.
Got too much on my mind.
Weather and a woman.

How did I slip?
Who touched my shit?
Been grinding five to four.
So busy, I need more.
Open my heart's front door.
Weather and a woman.

Confusing, hot, complicated.
Used to be not complicated.
Love, dance, run. Favorite months.
We don't go out there these days,
those afternoons, they've sailed away.

Sunshine gets complicated.
I swear, today and I melted.
Miles away, don't touch my shit.
If we want it, we've already won.
Weather and a woman.

All of my chips.
Deal me more shit.
Been yearning for a smile.
Brought home like it's in style.
Rock with me for a while.
Weather and a woman.

Fell on a blip.
I lost my shit.
Been years since I had it.
Screens projecting static.
Stuck up in my attic.
Weather and a woman.

Where is my ship?
Love, up in this attic.
Love up in my attic.
Make silence, not static.
Sweet dreams, not static.
I always thought I was melting.

Not Forgetting

Flippity, drippity, skipping me, stop.
Thinking then blinking then shrinking that thought.

Freaking out, speaking out, leaking what's clear.
Churning then learning then burning all fear.

Staring down at the line between reason and rhyme.
Giving another person another piece of our time.
Walking a whole life, never reading a book,
penning your own, though constantly shook.

I lay me out to dry and wonder what I'm sweating.
I prayed once and must've been misunderstood.
Could've sworn that's not what I asked for.
Come to think of it, I never asked for anything.
I say I'd pray again one day,
she'd stay, we'd stroll on all the beaches.
I lay me out and hope I'm not forgetting.

Sqwuakity, talkity, watch us grow old.
Writing this, fighting this blight-singing soul.

Sanctity, pranks on me, thanks to my luck.
Worry me, hurry me, don't give a fuck.

Pray to myself and misunderstand what I say.
My anchor's out there leaving, feel it's floating away.
It was all coming together and bursting apart.
Skipping, circles inside my mind
and all they saw was art.

Later on, when the suns show their faces,
I'll go walk outside to stop inside pacing.
Probably wish it was still around -
a smile not seen in a while, back on the ground,
I'll lay me out tonight and hope I don't forget it.

Lessons For This

Why read a book?
Someone's ideas. Somebody made up everything,
may as well make up my own.
I guess I've gotten used to this, I gotta get on the road.
Three more days and I'll be moving mountains.

Taught myself, why it's different.
Taught or given, gifts get thrifted.
I don't believe there are lessons for this,
not until I'm through and look back.

Maybe I'd write it down,
how to avoid the most bizarre stuff around.
Don't think they'd believe it.
Nobody'd believe it.
How is it so different?

Half myself, what is that?
Am I the ball? Am I the bat?
In control from different directions.
I sail, I come and I go, bare with me.
Gets windy.

Why read a book?
Somebody made up everything.
Figure it out as I go,
what other way to know for certain that I know?

Song To Me

I will rock my soul.
I will be like me.
Do everything I want.
Tomorrow I'll be free.

I will not grow old.
Always be just me.
Say everything I want.
I don't know what that means.

I go this way, you go yours.
These days I know I need me more,
and I don't know what you're doing.

A chair outside when nothing lines up.
Hide inside 'til I open up
and I'll write a song to me.

I will take the blows.
I will follow me.
Go everywhere I want,
I will take the lead.

I will not be sold,
I will keep to me.
Get everything I want.
A lot less than you need.

Everything I see will be a song I read.
Everything will be a song to me.

Queens Won't Sway

Life's tried to win my entire life.

I play every day, I write every night.
Throw it all at me at once and I'll still stay.
I'll probably go crazy, maybe lose my way.
Kings are slaves, Queens won't sway.
Life's just a game I continue to play.

Taking pieces who weren't meant to be taken.
People piecing me together so I can see what happens.

These days I cannot fade.
These days I want to play.

Cards or hearts? Never known how to play.
Throw it all at me at once, don't think I'll fade.
See me breaking, you're sure I'll lose my way.
I've got people who keep me together these days.
I care about dreaming, so I continue to stay.

I stopped talking the other night.
Life's easier to play than to fight.
Life's tried to win my entire life.
If you'd allow me to be me, I'd be useful.
I just wanna see what happens,
so I continue to play.

I cannot fade.
All my doors opened on the exact same day.
I just wanna see what happens.

Push Me

Mend me, bend me, break me.
Push me 'til I'm the dumbest person in the room.
Surround me with genius.
Push me out of place so I'll feel easy
and one day, maybe, get some rest.

Elephants ruffle the feathers outside the room.
How'd the future come so soon?
What happened to the weather?
Everybody's talking.

I came down and they all left the ground.

Fix me, kick me, lift me.
Pull me 'til I'm much farther than I am right now.
Surround me with loving.
Pull me to that place where it's all easy
and it stays that way for a while.

Spill Sometimes

She pulled him out, she fell right in.
She told him just to let her swim.

The coffee spilled, it always does,
and she got mad because he was.

Sometimes it all spills a little
when you're swimming upstream.
Rarely is it good if you don't ever dream.
Always be open when fighting your wars.
You can be busy and still be bored.
Follow your heart and find fresh air,
but running away will never get you there.

Anyway, back to his morning.
Flick, sip, morning, say hello.
That was his every morning.

The coffee's fresh, it always is.
He likes her heart and she likes his.

He sends her words for her to hold
at times when she has lost control.

Sometimes it all spills a little
when you're swimming all the way upstream.

Stacked Storms

Below your toes, just above your waist.
Inside, find bottom. You dig in, escape.
Under the clouds, ahead of the night.
Outside, jump in. Take the biggest dive.

To the right of those, and just above a bed,
beneath the thoughts that crawl inside your head,
you walk a trail on top of this shelf.
Looking down, you're smiling at yourself.

Show whites through a storm that I just got out of.
Small, but built so strong that she's never over.
I basically ate up the trail.
Me, messily.
Wade carefully.
Stone's slippery.
Focus your eyes and feel you breathe.
You and you are all you need.
I left all of the signs.

Take it so slow. Walk through all the waste.
You'll feel the bottom before you escape.
Just past the marker that I colored in,
where you see the light is not where it ends.

Grind your way out, find familiar touch.
If you get that lost, you'll learn so much.
One day you walk in and realize you're fine,
you see that you've still got all of your time.

Under an ear, deep inside a heart,
I take in what critics would call art.
On your rooftop, four feet go sing to stars.
We can see that we've come so far.
Never looking back.
All those storms that someone stacked.

Really After

The silent type, though full of thunder.
Not naive, but so much younger.
Her roots will weave and wade in wonder.
What are you really after?

Close a book and think out loud.
Give a look, don't make a sound
as trees and brooks drown with the clouds.
What are you really after?

You just go until you fly.
If we close our eyes
and there's no one else around us,
then nobody knows what happens around us.
I found it and the world opened up.
You just go until you fly.

One day you wake up to more.
Pieces break up and you're more.
You realize these streams have no shore
and you chase what you're really after.

What are you really after?

My Own Gospel

A little peace and quiet,
let the leaves stay.
No need to always be blowing them away.

They're leaves.
They're like me,
they'll come back.

I gotta write my own gospel.
I've never understood
anything I should have read in a book.

A little peace and quiet,
let the dust stay.
No need to always be throwing things away.

It's dust.
It's like me,
won't settle.

I gotta write my own gospel.

My God

My god is a song.
Off-notes, letting demons throw down.
Working toward my favorite version.

My god is a song.
Skipped hits, little lies for no reason.
Working toward an early version.

Sometimes the song is a moment.
Sometimes the song is this life.
Sometimes the song gets forgotten.
Sometimes it's something I write.

Better - never real, only preference.
Play through this lifetime with reverence.
There's work to be done, but I'm learning
and I've always liked this part.

My god is a song.
Hit peaks, doing fascinating things.
Working toward my most beautiful version.

My god is a song.
Heart-notes are handwritten letters.
Working toward what's,
to my ears,
a perfect version.

Starts so slow,
gets weird,
then whispers.

Play it gently.
Play it, beautiful.

How Many Stories?

Maybe I've had too much time to think.

Moral of the story,
most all of these stories have to have an end.

Maybe I've had too much time to think.
Maybe too much time since my last drink.

Immortal was a story.
Portals to glory they want you to believe in.

Maybe I've had too much time to think.
Maybe too much time since my last drink.
Surfacing colors starting to shrink.

Her life's another story.
Tragedy, glory. I'm always on the same page.

Maybe I've had too much time to think.
Maybe too much time since my last drink.
Surfacing colors starting to shrink.
Took a look at the sun, unintentional wink.

We're all riding out a story.
It's all hiding in a spotlight on a stage.

What if we share stories?
What if it's all one story?
Don't tell me how it ends.
Somebody's writing a story, and
somebody is confused.

Sometimes I feel like a warrior.
Sometimes I get the feeling
we share the same story.

Unfinished

Half hundred half read books smoking on his floor.
Staring, wondering how they would have ended.

Doesn't finish anything.
He kicked his wheel, built it up and she wrecked it.
Make way for this gem,
ice cream cones come true after he trashes them.
What if it's all worth the hassle,
and what if he never finds out?

Truth and simple lead to stronger.
This listen-to list is only getting longer.
'I finish nothing, so nothing ever ends.
And I can't go there,
because I don't know where she went.'

Do you hear angels sing?
What a deal, scored some records for my devil.
Remembering bliss,
I screamed, 'I'll wait forever just to feel this.'
What is waiting, but the freedom
to work this life into whatever we desire?

So, we crawl, then we run
with time and the sun on our shoulders.
After fall, winter comes
with the same exact sun, but it's colder.

And we shake, then we breathe
in time, with the wings on our shoulders.
After all this, we see
we're like angels who sing, but we're older.

Puts out books to see where he left off.
To know how they got older,
to see that things got mended.
These stories he let smolder.
To know how they all ended.

Circus

Put on a smile,
dance through the day
'til four in the morning,
it won't go away.

When it's too much,
and we break down for days,
somehow, we get through
this lifelong ballet.

Surrounded by clowns,
our purpose deserts us.
We try to remember
that life's just a circus

Questions to ask. They're just waiting to talk.
The elephant was on the table.
Yeah all of it was on the table.

The man walks on glass beneath the water.
The people watch and they believe. We leave.
Crawling up the ladder we leap to perception's trapeze.

Now how do you see it?
Now how does it seem?

It's a circus, but it's our circus.
This is our ballet, this is our circus.

The Man

Arms are disconnected,
can't feel them from my head.
The voices never stop,
still remember what you said.

A scream into a feather
that no one ever hears.
Feel the future coming,
that feeling disappears.

The man
in the dress
on the throne
on the wall,
well, he's not really here,
but he sees it all.

Light a yellow candle,
white bugs climb black walls.
Man, my brain is broken,
toes clench into a ball

Curl up and calm down,
the whispers start to fade.
Release my soul and burn
the paintings that you made.

Scratches on the corner,
four eyes on a shelf.
Remember you said 'maybe'?
Can't get up by myself.

Fall out of a memory,
my nerves come unwound
The music's getting louder,
the ceiling's coming down.

But he sees it all.
But he hears it all.
But he feels it all.

Wonder Out A Window

Grinning, spinning on a tube.
Smile and say, 'what is it with you?'
Gotta bring me with me when I move.

Slipping, tripping on the moon.
Lean in, laugh, and roll off the roof.
Something always happens when we lose.

And I can hear two songs right now.
And I'm sliding sideways while I write right now.
Scribbling on a road, headed home.
Any road'll go somewhere.
Why wouldn't I wonder out the window?

Spray painted halo preaching to me.

Prying, flying on a dream.
Keeping happy, harder than it seems.
Gotta live some grit if we're ever gonna gleam.

Sitting, knitting up a scene.
Still standing, changing what it means.
Gotta get together if this feeling's gonna flee.

Preacher, spray paint halo, you don't know
anything more than what I wonder out a window.

Buried

In some ways, it's already yesterday.
I don't know how I made it.
I got buried.
I dug in. Got dug out by people I dig.
Pulled out by people I love.
Why do people get buried?
Wake up one day and for one year, more.
Buried.
More. It gets scary.
Everyday, being buried.
Surrounded by so much love.
You know it,
but you know knowing isn't feeling.
Feel it?
The worst feeling is not feeling it.
I got buried.
I don't know how I made it.
If I've made it.
Yet.
I don't bet against me.
Or you. People who stay true.
They've been buried.
They say it builds character.
I'm surrounded by characters.
Seen both sides.
If you haven't dug in, been pulled out,
lost it, been buried, knew and not felt
new feelings they told you about -
I'll just never understand.
No envy.
It's so hard and it happens
and we make it and
it's worth it.
We're heroes and we don't know it.
We feel it.
The strongest people I know
got thrown back to getting buried.
Too many times.

You're moving, they're dying, leaving,
driving, flying, work's crazy, more driving,
you're lost and found.
Buried at the bottom of the lost and found.
Your heart pounds.
Your heart beats so loud,
it keeps you from sleeping
and there aren't enough hours or days
to do everything and nothing at all
and you just
want
to
sleep.
Dream of when it's over.
Settles down.
Feet back on the ground.
And it happens.
Somehow, it happens.
People (you) pull you out.
Pushed them all away
and think you've gone insane, then
it gets clear and they're all still here.
'Happy you made it.'
Nothing ever makes sense,
but somehow it happens.
You wake up.
Mirror, own eyes, realize,
open up, appreciate love you've found.
It surrounds.
You love how it all sounds.
And it's loud.
And you're proud.
And that's allowed.
No lights and it's bright.
You know? You feel it?
It feels like just yesterday
and you're humbled.
In some ways, it's already yesterday.
You don't know how you made it.
You got buried.

At least that's how I felt.
Partially buried now, myself.

Between The Lines

Don't know how to say this
so it's stuck between the lines,
spilled on a page.
Words are easier when they're written down.

When everything's perfect I will throw it away
to search for different and bet on better days.
I've had enough sunshine, I'll go out digging for rain,
and he said maybe sometimes we all just need a little pain.

Run it into the ground when it all seems too easy,
then I'll rise up again and you'll never believe me.

And when it all comes undone,
I'll close my eyes to hear what he's singing.
I'll go back to the ball
for a while to unwind,
and take note of the moment when I come across my mind.

All the brainwash and stories, and I really don't care.
I'm a little too smart and a little too scared.
They say it's the only constant, so this may sound a little strange
my biggest fear in life is that things will never change.

I'll blow it all up and I'll sink my own ship.
Man, I know there's more to life than living like this.

And when it all comes undone,
I'll close my eyes to hear what he's singing.
I'll go back to the ball
for a while to unwind,
and take note of the moment when I come across my mind.

Just a little more, I won't care what I'm paying.
Won't care what you said, did you think I was staying?
A yearning in my heart and a fire in my eyes.
Does that side of this mountain have blue or gray skies?

One of these days when I abandon this ship,
I'll look back and forget that I had nights like this.

Overwhelmed, Easy

I'll trash that whole day now.
I'm so clear in the mirror and it's so foggy out,
I can't see a thing.

Sliding sideways between three white lines,
songs about your shirt humming in my ears,
waving past the window, hoping you sleep tonight.

I'll leave those old ways now.
I'm so close to my ghosts, they don't ever shout,
only have to whisper.

I've been walking forever
and we're not where we all wanna be.
I know how to get there,
but who would listen to me?

Ride on next to the night, tired treads taking flight.
The wind in this city isn't what it used to be.
But, we both know, one day it's gonna happen.

We stood there for ten years,
what do you remember?
I don't remember it all.
I love your love like rooftops in the rain.
The ways certain things branch out in your brain,
reaching for joy, you, and your tomorrows.
Patience and love, and it'll always happen.

Sliding sideways between the lines.
Overwhelmed and easy.

Sometimes I Forget

Sometimes I forget that
beneath all the bad days,
to the left of the lost ones,
above where I feel fear,
beyond how things seem and how things are,
down near days when you're not here,
days when music's all I hear,
past the broken promise people,
on top of the thoughts gone
and thoughts wrong,
inside, on top of weeks spent inside,
on top of the weeks with no one to talk to,
between the confusion of you and me,
beneath my bones, my filled-up heart
and tucked into the cushion of my soul,

I am happy.

Bounce Back

I'm so good at walking. Walking's what I do.
When I need to stretch my thoughts,
footprints make them move.

I'm so good at falling. Falling's what I do.
When I find my mind is strong,
my face hits my shoes.

Another bounce back.
A float with a best friend.
Another breath to free what's been inside of me.
A chance to see those eyes dancing again.
I am not rebelling. I am done surviving.
I know there's no telling, I am just alive and
I'm looking for answers.
Another bounce back.

I'm so good at crawling. Crawling's what I do.
Time, it likes to pummel me,
so I strut two by two.

I'm so good at flying. Flying's what I do.
Earth's not built for hearts like this,
so I fly past the moon.

Always here, no matter when.
Did you get the thought I sent?
Did you hear the thought I heard?
Will you listen for the words meant for you?
I'm not lost again.

The Same

You begin, you only listen.
You begin, you haven't missed it.
You begin, you'll be ok.
Without expectations, you won't go astray.

You be young, you have some fun now.
You be young, you have no trouble.
You be young, you live all day.
Wade in the moment and you'll pave the way.

You be fine, you always make it.
You be fine, you never breaking.
You be fine, you can be strange.
No time for normal, and it's not today.

You be wise, you sell your castle.
You be wise, you use my shadow.
You be wise, you walk away.
You follow your heart, so your head won't sway.

and there's no more dismay.
and you can't find too late.
it's fortune and it's fate
that you negotiate.
what if they're the same?
you walk away.
you can be strange.
you live all day.
you'll be ok.
I think we're the same.

Morning Drive

I wake up,
Pour warm, iced, coffee.
Go for my drive.
It's the morning.

Windows down,
the fresh air suits me.
Turn up my songs,
it's my morning.

I've seen children running around.
I've seen people laughing out loud.
I've seen balloons out in the distance.
Do they see me on the ground?

Cacti bloom, water moves,
brand new shoes and I move too.
The sun slept in, so it could be a long day.

All these signs,
the stopping slows me.
Missed my target,
but, I've got all morning.

Take my time
and do what I need.
My life is today,
and it's still morning.

Who's Painting?

One day,
I'd love to live
where the fringe of the sea collides with the sky.
Discover where those colors went, who's painting?
Don't dissolve these. Live where all those colors went,
out by the toes of the sky.

Yesterday may be the same as tomorrow.
The way purple plays with water.
Unzip this ceiling, fill in the sky,
out where the colors and ocean collide.

Where I'll spend my time.
Dip my toes in turquoise.
Where I'll spend my time.
Colors and tides gently colliding.

Seasons Swing

Balcony
under me.
Live and see,
go listening.

Out of reach
on the beach.
Wondering
if waves are free.

Mountains left craters,
didn't know where to turn.
Oceans ran to rivers,
only to watch them burn.

Flying feathers fled
before the day went back to bed.
In the sand,
I just feel different.

Distance leaves
before me.
Lost at sea,
then glistening.

Silent feet
on a beach
watching these
seasons swing.

Just Enough

He was watching from the corner,
thinkin', 'I don't have enough.'
She was dancing like she used to.
Singin', 'boy, you're way too much.'

She was dancing by the bad door.
Singin', 'I've got way too much.'
He was watching like he used to.
Thinkin', 'love, you're just enough.'

Belting movie tunes just before Halloween.
Singing.
They wonder if they remember,
knowing they'll always understand.

Roaring, making moves.
Please act as though you never knew.
Quiet, napalm news he'd previously received,
so he understood what was happening.

He was floating in her freedom,
thinkin', 'I don't have a clue.'
She was jumping on an old bed
singin', 'boy, you know it's you.'

She was living like a rebel
singin', 'what happened to you?'
He was writing on an old bed
thinkin', 'love, I left the clues.'

Worn, but built with patience to barrel past anything.
Desert, midwest, mazes, phases, following, falling,
or chasing every dream, or everything it seems.
Singing.
They'll always understand.

Sounds Like The Radio

Give me a house, woman.
Woman, give me a home.
Give me a place to sleep inside where I won't feel all alone.

Give me your love, lady.
Lady, give me a home.
Give me a place to rest my head and a kiss before you go.

It's fall outside through the window and she sounds like the radio.
Life is easy, blue breezes breathing.
Fall in love, don't say a word and eventually it occurs to her
how it was meant to be.

It's all outside through the window.

Give me a key, teacher.
Teacher won't you let me in?
Let me in before you go and watch our lives as they begin.

Give me your eyes mister.
Mister, see what I have seen?
Mister says my eyes have seen some things
wilder than your wildest dreams.

It falls outside through the window.
It's how it was meant to be, but it all feels make believe.

Seeking Through Static

Stars circle around us
'til they run out of space.
Hit walls before ground,
and set sail at a steadier pace.

Tell me I'm not getting any younger,
or a lot more that I've never known.
Tell me I'm a fool to always wonder,
or something else I've never been told.

Tell me that I don't know what I'm doing,
or anything that never crossed my mind.
Tell me that I'm crazy for not snoozing,
or something else that wastes my time.

Stars hurdle the ground
until they fall on their face.
Burn out, then come down
and stumble in with familiar grace.

Discover it all as we go.
Everything I learned today,
was a few things that my radio played.
Stars come down and find their place.

Turning dials for a while,
seeking more than static.
My mind's on a star and I can't get any signal.
Like there's a heart up in my attic.
We're never far from where we could be going.
Watching the FM spin again.
Two stars time-lapse down a dirt road.
Seeking more than static.

Window Pane

When I walk to your window,
I see myself looking in.
Moving drops of melted snow
to find a fire burning
near your warm and calming glow.

You see you outside of old frames.
You see your life moving in.
Icy roads, you dream of leaving.
Memories filtering
the cold air you've been breathing.

The sky slides softly into the ground.
You're my old song, you're my favorite sound.
The sky could crash when you're around
and I'd know I am fine.

Why can't I control time?
I'd feel I am fine.

Longing breath on the window,
you slowly fade away.
Fingerprints to pane. I see belief
that life will be better
out there, just beyond the rain.

Time fixing up the old walls,
mudding memories away.
Grey tee shirt and paint, please roll to me.
Your eyes smile and I breathe
as the snow becomes the rain.

South. City bound in the morning.
We could use a little rain.
I'm more of me when it's both of us,
and I can only see both of us
through this window pane.

The sky could hit the ground.
You should be around.
Do you know you are fine?
Just take a little time.

I've always loved your rain.

Conductor In The Caboose

Two leaves danced off a tree
to get down, see what's out there.
Tangoing, different speeds,
to build crowns, get some fresh air.

Two drops left on a train
to move on, felt all they'd seen.
Conductor, in front of rain,
sings his song, humming, 'I know what you mean.'

Throwing more love to the fire,
melt steel and leave storms behind us.
A tired man in a cap tracks back to the caboose
and sits down for the first time in a while.
Two drops behind him.
Raindrops on railroads.
Conductor stuck under a life he's left,
and the rain just rolls up his windshield.

Two hands twirl on a clock
to call up perspiring rays.
Dialing time 'til it talks,
singing songs, humming, 'to sunnier days.'

Two rails run to the west
to slow down, breathe, and feel free.
Gamboling through bad and best,
like two leaves dancing off of a tree.

Lining up, suddenly.
Dancing the same direction.

Looking Back At Wild

She was standing there,
eyeing me down, smiling in the corner.
Looking back, I should've warned her that
I leave myself at times.
Looking back, I think I did.

I always saw all this coming.
I always saw it back then.
We always whispered of madness.
We always did it for them.

We never listened to no one.
We never listen, just leave.
We only hear what we want to.
We only do what we please.

Steel starts spinning on the rails,
but the train's not goin' nowhere.
Wright's on the stereo.
Life's on, it's staring us all in the face.
You could make it easy but you can't stop the race.
Won't stop the race.
Steel starts spinning.
My wheels start moving.
They'd roll back up the mountain,
but they can't stop the race.

Trains were waiting there,
puddles from pain stood still on the corner.
Stumbling back, she tried to warn him that
she must do what she needs.
Looking back, I think she did.

We didn't think it could happen.
We didn't know we'd be fine.
We should've lived for the moment.
We should've let us trust time.

He brings his bag full of brilliance.
She brings her bag full of wild.
They make a home out of simple.
They make a home out of smiles.

Looking back, I think they did.

Index

Love you, Mom

www.ingramcontent.com/pod-product-compliance
Lightning Source LLC
LaVergne TN
LVHW020512100826
845148LV00003B/764

* 9 7 8 1 7 3 5 0 4 3 4 0 1 *